ROALD DAHL

BEASTLY & BEWILDERING

WORDS

Original text by
Roald Dahl

Illustrated by
Quentin Blake

Compiled by
Kay Woodward

OXFORD
UNIVERSITY PRESS

GRRR...

Some words are so incredibly beastly that they make your hair stand on end. Others are bewildering enough to make you gawp until a grown-up asks you to close your mouth, please. And because Roald Dahl loved to **WOW** his readers, his stories overflow with words like these which are guaranteed to do just that.

But, WAIT.

Did you know that 'beastly' isn't just a way of saying that something is horrid or unpleasant? Long ago, it actually meant 'like a beast'. This happens with other adjectives too. For example, 'bubbly' doesn't just mean that something is filled with bubbles. The word can also be used to describe someone who's super cheerful.

Now just imagine if some of the **beastliest** and **most bewildering** words ever had been herded together into one handy book. Well, guess what . . . they have. Even better, this is that book! And whether you know every single Roald Dahl story off by heart or you're saving them all for a very rainy day, prepare to find out more about the wild words inside. There are top tips for making your own writing unbelievably awesome too.

Take a deep breath and prepare yourself for a totally **beastly** – and **bewildering** – time.

— Kay Woodward

CONTENTS

BEASTLY BEASTS

Not all beasts are beastly.
(The Muggle-Wumps are terribly nice.) But
some beasts are way more beastly
than others. And a few of the beasts
in Roald Dahl's stories are beastly
beyond belief. Take the **Vermicious
Knids**, for example.*

These space villains are so wickedly
wiggly that even Willy Wonka is
terrified of them!

*'From fifty yards away, a fully grown
Vermicious Knid could stretch out its neck and
bite your head off without even getting up!'*
— CHARLIE AND THE GREAT GLASS ELEVATOR

vermicious

adjective

It might sound incredibly odd, but the word vermicious was NOT invented by Roald Dahl. It's actually 100% real! Vermicious means 'worm-like' and comes from *vermis* – the Latin for 'worm'.

Knid is a different story, however. This bizarre word was totally made up by the world's greatest storyteller. When you read 'knid' aloud, don't forget that the k is NOT silent, like the k in knife and knee. You'll need to say ALL the letters: k-n-i-d.

Why not invent your own beastly beast and name it? Then make up your own crazy pronunciation too!

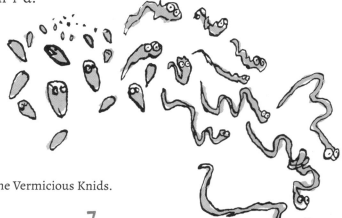

* Someone PLEASE take the Vermicious Knids.

7

The Enormous Crocodile
is another truly
BEASTLY BEAST.

'I'm off to find a yummy child for lunch. Keep listening and you'll hear the bones go crunch!'
— THE ENORMOUS CROCODILE

STERN WARNING:

If you are a child, you are strongly advised to avoid the
Enormous Crocodile, especially if it's nearly lunchtime.
And if your name is Billy, don't go ANYWHERE near the
Terrible Bloodsuckling Toothpluckling Stonechuckling Spittler
or the Red-Hot Smoke-Belching Gruncher either.

... the **Red-Hot Smoke-Belching Gruncher**...
*can smell out a human or a Minpin or any other
animal from ten miles away. Then he gallops
towards it at terrific speed.*
— BILLY AND THE MINPINS

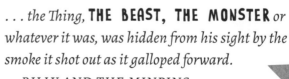

... *the Thing,* **THE BEAST, THE MONSTER** *or
whatever it was, was hidden from his sight by the
smoke it shot out as it galloped forward.*
— BILLY AND THE MINPINS

9

Nouns can be a little dull and boring on their own. But add adjectives – like beastly, for example – and they burst into life magnificently. Here are more awful adjectives for you to choose from.

cruel

objectionable

loathsome

awful

disagreeable

abominable

unfair

horrible

hateful

mean

vile

terrible

detestable

unpleasant

rotten

shocking

foul

Esio Trot! What are YOU doing here? You're not even a tiny bit beastly. Please whizz to page 16 at once! (Or shuffle really slowly, if you absolutely insist.)

He crept on his toes towards the ugly brutes. They were still snoring loudly. They looked **REPULSIVE, FILTHY, DIABOLICAL.**

— THE BFG

Can you think of any more REALLY NASTY adjectives?

Creature CHARACTERS

There's one very big difference between real animals and the animals in Roald Dahl's stories. Real animals act like, well . . . animals. Meanwhile, characters like Fantastic Mr Fox and the Enormous Crocodile act like humans!

When we say animals or things behave like humans, it is called:

ANTHROPOMORPHISM

Show off to your friends by dropping this splendiferous word into conversations.
Show off to teachers by learning to spell it too!
(It's easier than it looks.)

MEET FANTASTIC MR FOX!

Here are just three of the many, many ways in which Mr Fox shows that he is different to the average fox.

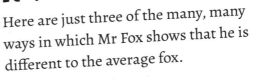

HE CAN SPEAK.

'Well, my darling, what shall it be this time? A plump chicken from Boggis? A duck or a goose from Bunce? Or a nice turkey from Bean?'

— FANTASTIC MR FOX

HE WEARS CLOTHES.

Take a moment to admire Mr Fox's dinner jacket, waistcoat and necktie. Aren't they elegant? Aren't they divine?

HE BURPS.

'This delicious meal . . .' he began, then he stopped. In the silence that followed, he let fly a tremendous belch.

— FANTASTIC MR FOX

Gosh, how rude.

Here are more amazing anthropomorphic characters to look out for in Roald Dahl's stories. This Monkey can sing and dance!

'We are the Window-Cleaners!' sang out the Monkey.
'We will polish your glass
Till it's shining like brass
And it sparkles like sun on the sea!
We are quick and polite,
We will come day or night,
The Giraffe and the Pelly and me!'
— THE GIRAFFE AND THE PELLY AND ME

Have you ever seen a duck wear an apron or sleep in a bed or play with a model train set? These ducks do.

The ducks were walking in a line to the door of the
Greggs' house, swinging their arms and holding
their beaks high in the air.
— THE MAGIC FINGER

14

The creatures inside the Giant Peach are VERY good at arguing like human beings.

'You have a lot of boots,' James murmured.
'I have a lot of legs,' the Centipede answered proudly.
'And a lot of feet. One hundred, to be exact.'
'There he goes again!' the Earthworm cried, speaking for the first time. 'He simply cannot stop telling lies about his legs! He doesn't have anything like a hundred of them! He's only got forty-two!'
— JAMES AND THE GIANT PEACH

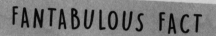

FANTABULOUS FACT

The English word 'centipede' comes from the French word *centipède*. This, in turn, comes from the Latin words *centum* (which means 'a hundred') and *ped* (this means 'foot'). But different species of centipede actually have different numbers of legs. Some have as few as thirty legs, while others have hundreds!

15

ESIO TROT, there you are!
Welcome to page 16.

Not all of Roald Dahl's creature characters behave like humans, of course. Like Esio Trot, for instance. He doesn't sing or stroll along or boast about how many legs he's got. He just moves **v-e-r-y s-l-o-w-l-y** and eats lettuce like, erm, well . . . like a tortoise. And that's because he IS a tortoise. So if you ever feel like writing a story about an animal, don't forget that it's completely acceptable for them to be exactly that – an animal.

However, there is something remarkable about Esio Trot's name.
'Esio Trot is simply tortoise spelled backwards,' Mr Hoppy said. *'Look at it.'*
'So it is,' Mrs Silver said.
— ESIO TROT

Now try working out what these magic words mean. They are written in the style of Esio Trot, so all you have to do is read them backwards!

ESIO TROT, ESIO TROT, ⬅

TEG REGGIB REGGIB! ⬅

EMOC NO, ESIO TROT, ⬅

WORG PU, FFUP PU, TOOHS PU! ⬅

Why not use this style yourself to write secret messages to your friends? Only REAL Roald Dahl fans will be able to decode them!

No matter how far you travel or how hard you search, some creatures can ONLY be found inside a Roald Dahl story.

MINPINS are tiny creatures who try their hardest to avoid being gobbled up by the **Red-Hot Smoke-Belching Gruncher**.

Perhaps Minpins got their name because they are mini and as small as pins?

'We are the Minpins,' the tiny man said, 'and we own this wood.'
— BILLY AND THE MINPINS

OOMPA-LOOMPAS work in Willy Wonka's chocolate factory in exchange for chocolate, which is their favourite food. A tuba is a brass instrument that makes a wonderfully deep OOMPAH sound. Maybe this is why the Oompa-Loompas like music?

'Listen!' whispered Charlie. 'Listen, Grandpa!
The Oompa-Loompas in the boat outside are starting to sing!'
— CHARLIE AND THE CHOCOLATE FACTORY

18

GNOOLIES are invisible and deadly creatures that live under the Earth's surface in Minusland.

'You can't see Gnoolies, my boy. You can't even feel them . . . until they puncture your skin . . . then it's too late. They've got you.'

— CHARLIE AND THE GREAT GLASS ELEVATOR

Gnooly sounds a little like ghoul — an evil spirit or phantom.

Jellyfish and BULLFROGS

Sometimes, the best way to describe a human being – whether it's the way they look, sound, move or act – is by likening them to . . . an animal!

*Aunt Sponge, fat and pulpy as a **jellyfish**, came waddling up behind her sister to see what was going on.*
— JAMES AND THE GIANT PEACH

20

Grandma Georgina, in her red flannel nightgown with two skinny bare legs sticking out of the bottom, was trumpeting and spitting like a **rhinoceros**.

— CHARLIE AND THE GREAT GLASS ELEVATOR

At the mention of this word, Miss Trunchbull's face turned purple and her whole body seemed to swell up like a **bullfrog's**.

— MATILDA

Mr Hazell would strut about like a **peacock** *welcoming them.*

— DANNY THE CHAMPION OF THE WORLD

FANTABULOUS FACT

A simile is a phrase that describes something in a vivid way. It does this by comparing it with another thing that is very, very different. Similes are easy to recognize because they use the words 'as' or 'like'.

A **metaphor** is a superb way of adding pizzazz to a description. It can be used to compare two things that are almost completely different, while being alike in a very small way. It's also a great opportunity to let your imagination run **WILD**.

The Bloodbottler was a gruesome sight . . . Craggy yellow teeth stuck out between the two purple frankfurter lips, and **rivers of spit** *ran down over the chin.*
— THE BFG

The Bloodbottler doesn't really have lips made of **German sausage**, of course. But that's what they sort of look like. Neither does the Bloodbottler have life-sized rivers of spit running down his chin. (That would be redunculous. He'd be drenched in no time.) These dribbles do look like rivers – just very, very titchy ones.

Mr Hoppy turned and ran from the balcony into the living-room, jumping on tip-toe like a ballet dancer between the **sea of tortoises** *that covered the floor.*

— ESIO TROT

Alert! It's clearly not an actual sea, because seas are filled with water, not small, slow, creatures with shells.

Some verbs – words that describe actions – are often used to describe how animals move.

scuttle · slink · trot · gallop · bound · leap · spring · crawl · crouch · stampede · lumber · waddle · trot · stamp · stalk · pounce

'You call that walking?' cried the Centipede. 'You're a slitherer, that's all you are!

You just slither along!'

'I glide,' said the Earthworm, primly.

— JAMES AND THE GIANT PEACH

Suddenly there was a tremendous whooshing noise. It was Humpy-Rumpy, the Hippopotamus. He came **crashing** and **snorting** out of the jungle. His head was down low and he was galloping at a terrific speed.

— THE ENORMOUS CROCODILE

Here's some wondercrump news! There isn't a rule that says these verbs are ONLY for animals. They can be used for chocolate-factory owners too (and other human beings, of course). So why not squeeze more of them into your own stories, like Roald Dahl? They are SO much more imaginative than plain old walking.

'Here we are!' cried Mr Wonka, trotting along in front of the group.

— CHARLIE AND THE CHOCOLATE FACTORY

Dogs **BARK** , **GROWL** and **HOWL** .

Cats **HISS** and **MIAOW** .

These animal noises might all look very different to each other, but they are alike in a remarkable way.

They are **onomatopoeic** words

(say on-o-mat-o-pee-ik)

which means that they sound like the thing they describe. If you want to find out whether a word is onomatopoeic or not, simply say it aloud, in a

REALLY BIG VOICE.

Practise with these beastly sounds! And if grown-ups complain, simply ask them very politely to shush. (That's onomatopoeic too.)

grunt   snort   snuffle   whimper   neigh

whinny   croak   whine   bellow   snarl   roar

gobble   twitter   drone

These words can also be used to describe the ways that human beings speak.

Captain Lancaster sat up front at his desk, gazing suspiciously round the class with his watery-blue eyes. And even from the back row I could hear him snorting and snuffling through his nose like dog outside a rabbit hole.

— DANNY THE CHAMPION OF THE WORLD

Beastly TALES

Can you imagine what it might be like to **turn into an animal**? What if you grew feathers or fur or shrank until you were very, very small indeed? Do you think this would be tremendously exciting or more shocking than learning that all you could eat for the rest of your life was cheese? These characters found out . . .

28

Case Study: BRUNO JENKINS

Suddenly he had a tail . . .
And then he had whiskers . . .
Now he had four feet . . .
It was all happening so quickly . . .
It was a matter of seconds only . . .
And all at once he wasn't there any more . . .
A small brown mouse . . .
Was running around on the table top . . .
— THE WITCHES

metamorphosis *noun*

This is when something or someone
changes into something completely
different. In Franz Kafka's very
short book called *Metamorphosis* he
wrote about a man who turns into a
gigantuous insect. **Eeeeeek.**

In fairy tales, it's not unusual for a character to be magically transformed into something entirely different, such as a beast or a frog or a swan. If they are really lucky, they will be magically transformed back into a human again at the end of the tale. (If they are unlucky, they won't.)

Now's your chance to write your own beastly fairy tale, using this handy guide to inspire you!

Think of a title for your fairy tale.

Choose your main characters.

(Don't forget to name them too!)

Now decide
upon a villain.

(We suggest inventing a
REALLY beastly one.)

Which character
will you magically
transform . . .?

And, more
importantly, WHY?

Even more importantly, what
will you turn them into?

(Helpful suggestions: a giant with
a hooked nose; a monstrous slug;
a tap-dancing squirrel.)

Will there be a happy ending?

YES!

NO!

31

Human BEASTS

If you dip into a dictionary*, you'll see that the definition of beast is 'an animal'. But a beast can also mean 'a very cruel person'. Roald Dahl's stories are brimming with these horrigust beasts . . .

MR TWIT

. . . Mr Twit was a foul and smelly old man. He was also an extremely horrid old man . . .

— THE TWITS

THE TRUNCHBULL

Her face, I'm afraid, was neither a thing of beauty nor a joy for ever. She had an obstinate chin, a cruel mouth and small arrogant eyes.

— MATILDA

GEORGE'S GRANDMA

Most grandmothers are lovely, kind, helpful old ladies, but not this one. She spent all day and every day sitting in her chair by the window, and she was always complaining, grousing, grouching, grumbling, griping about something or other.

— GEORGE'S MARVELLOUS MEDICINE

* This is something that we highly recommend doing, JUST FOR FUN.

FARMER BOGGIS, FARMER BUNCE AND FARMER BEAN

Down in the valley there were three farms. The owners of these farms had done well. They were rich men. They were also nasty men. All three of them were about as nasty and mean as any men you could meet.

— FANTASTIC MR FOX

Some of Roald Dahl's magnificently mean characters are doubly beastly. They LOOK like animals too!

MR VICTOR HAZELL

He sat quite still in the seat of his Rolls-Royce, his tiny piggy eyes staring straight ahead. There was a smug superior little smile around the corners of his mouth.

— DANNY THE CHAMPION OF THE WORLD

MR WORMWOOD

Mr Wormwood was a small ratty-looking man whose front teeth stuck out underneath a thin ratty moustache.

— MATILDA

PSST. Switch Mr Wormwood's name around to discover another type of beast . . .

woodworm

34

RATTY and **PIGGY** are both adjectives inspired by animals that can be used to describe human beings instead. Here are more!

 catty – mean or cruel

 sheepish – when someone feels a little embarrassed because of something silly they've done

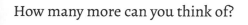 sluggish – slow or lazy movement (like a slug!)

How many more can you think of?

Q. When is a beast NOT a beast?

A. When it's a **brute** or a **monster** or a **savage** or a **barbarian** or an **ogre** or a **fiend** or a **demon** or a **devil**.

These words are all **synonyms** of beast.

A synonym is a word or phrase that means exactly or nearly the same as another word or phrase. Synonyms are a genius way of turning an everyday sentence into something truly memorable.

Phizz-whizzing tip!

Right now, you are probably wishing that there was some way of finding shiny new synonyms. Well, would you believe it? There is! A thesaurus is stuffed, packed, rammed, jammed and crammed full of splendiferous synonyms, helpfully arranged in alphabetical order.
So if you'd like to find a different way of saying something, open one up and look inside.

FANTABULOUS FACT

The word thesaurus comes from the Greek *thēsauros*, which means 'treasure house'. It's the perfect name for a book that's filled with dazzling and brilliantly wordy treasure!

How BEASTLY!

There's only one thing more beastly than a beastly character . . . and that's A BEASTLY CHARACTER WHO SAYS BEASTLY THINGS ABOUT BEASTS. (Grrrrr. How beastly!)

When the first letters of words next to or near each other start with the same letter, this is called **alliteration**.

'**Shrivelly** little **shrimp!**'
'**Grobby** little **grub!**'
— THE BFG

'You're a **barmy** old **bat!**' said Mr Wonka.
— CHARLIE AND THE GREAT GLASS ELEVATOR

'Oh **mince** my **maggots!**
Oh **swipe** my **swoggles!**'
— THE BFG

38

'My dear old trout!' Aunt Sponge cried out . . .
— JAMES AND THE GIANT PEACH

At first glance, it might look as if
Aunt Sponge is being kind to Aunt Spiker.
She does say, 'My dear . . .' But suggesting that
someone looks like a trout is NOT a compliment.
(Unless you're a fish, of course.) Here's another
beastly insult, this time from Mrs Twit . . .

*Silently, Mrs Twit came floating down. When she was about the
height of the house above Mr Twit, she suddenly called out at the
top of her voice, 'Here I come, you grizzly old grunion! . . .'*
— THE TWITS

phizz-whizzing fact

A grunion might sound like a made-up animal,
but it's actually REAL. Grunions are small thin
fish found off the coast of California.
They are excellent with chips.

GIANT-SIZED WARNING:
GIANTS ARE FAMOUS FOR USING GIGANTUOUS CURSES WHEN THINGS GO WRONG. DO NOT READ ANY FURTHER IF YOU ARE EASILY OFFENDED.

I'm **bopmuggered!**

I'm **crodsquinkled!**

I'm **fluckgungled!**

I'm **goosegruggled!**

I'm **gunzleswiped!**

The finest sight of all was to observe those nine hideous brutes squirming and twisting about . . . as they tried to free themselves from their ropes and chains.

'I is **flushbunkled!**' roared the Fleshlumpeater.

'I is **splitzwiggled!**' yelled the Childchewer.

'I is **swogswalloped!**' bellowed the Bonecruncher.

— THE BFG

Well, we did warn you. If YOU would like to curse like a giant, it's easy. Simply make up a brand new word. No one will have a CLUE what it means. They won't even know that you're angry! (Unless you've turned as purple as an aubergine and you're spitting and stamping and shaking your fist, of course. Then they might guess.)

41

It was the day I longed for and the day I dreaded. It was also the day of butterflies in the stomach except that they were worse than butterflies. They were snakes.

— DANNY THE CHAMPION OF THE WORLD

HELP. It's an emergency! Danny the Champion of the World has butterflies, no, **SNAKES** in his stomach! We need to get them out, AT ONCE. Except . . . we don't! These butterflies and snakes aren't real. (Phew. Everyone relax.)

'Butterflies in the stomach' is an **idiom** – a phrase that means something more than the simple meaning of the words. Here, it means that Danny has a fluttery, squirmy feeling in his stomach, not because it's full of butterflies and snakes, but because he's nervous.

Here are more animal idioms and their meanings.

To eat like a horse – to have a big appetite

Hold your horses – STOP RIGHT THERE

The elephant in the room – when there is a very large problem that everyone knows about, but pretends not to, because it might cause arguments or upset

To be the **cat's whiskers** or the **bee's knees** – to be utterly splendiferous

A **red herring** – a fake clue

A **one-trick pony** – someone who is very good at just one thing, but absolutely nothing else.

If we squeezed every animal idiom ever into this book, there would be no room for anything else. So listen out for them instead. You might be surprised at how many you hear.

PAILS OF SNAILS and LIZARDS' TAILS

WARNING: DO NOT READ THIS CHAPTER JUST BEFORE DINNER OR JUST AFTER BREAKFAST.

You might think that Brussels sprouts are utterly uckyslush or perhaps you would run a very long way to avoid a wobbly peach blancmange.* But what if you were faced with one of these beastly feasts?

'I've eaten fresh mudburgers by the greatest cooks there are,
. . . And pails of snails and lizards' tails,
And beetles by the jar.
(A beetle is improved by just a splash of vinegar.)'
— JAMES AND THE GIANT PEACH

eww!
disgustive!

---

* Alternatively, these might be your most favourite foods EVER.
In which case, yum! How delunctuous!

'Cabbage doesn't taste of anything without a few boiled caterpillars in it.'
— GEORGE'S MARVELLOUS MEDICINE

'I can mince it all up very fine and you won't even know the difference. Lovely slugburgers. Delicious.'
— THE MAGIC FINGER

yuck!

repulsive!

grobswitchy!

Which beastly recipe should you **NEVER** eat?
Formula 86 Delayed Action Mouse-Maker, of course!

'So you mix in the egg,' The Grand High Witch went on, 'and vun after
the other you also mix in the following items: the claw of a crrrabcrrruncher,
the beak of a blabbersnitch, the snout of a grrrobblesqvirt and the tongue of
a catsprrringer.'
— THE WITCHES

phizz-whizzing fact

Did you know that the world's greatest
playwright wrote about gruesome and gory
spell-making over four hundred years ago?

Fillet of a fenny snake,
In the cauldron boil and bake;
Eye of newt and toe of frog,
Wool of bat and tongue of dog,
Adder's fork and blind-worm's sting,
Lizard's leg and howler's wing . . .
— MACBETH BY WILLIAM SHAKESPEARE

Go on, invent your own truly terrible spell. Pop in the very worst ingredients you can think of. Make them so disgusterous that not even The Grand High Witch would touch them with her thin curvy claws.

Willy Wonka's recipe for **WONKA-VITE** isn't just rammed full of curious ingredients. It's positively popping with puns too!

like this

THE TRUNK (AND THE SUITCASE) OF AN ELEPHANT

Here, TRUNK obviously means an elephant's long, long nose.
Or does it . . ? NO. Roald Dahl has tricked you! This trunk is
actually the sort that is taken on a voyage with a suitcase. Oops!

Puns are wordy jokes that use **homonyms** – words that look
or sound alike, but have different meanings. First, it looks as
if a word means one thing and then – tadaaaaa! – it means
something else. Here are more:

THE HORN OF A COW (IT MUST BE A LOUD HORN)
THE HIDE (AND THE SEEK) OF A SPOTTED WHANGDOODLE
— CHARLIE AND THE GREAT GLASS ELEVATOR

Phizz-whizzing fact

Become a **champion** pun-spotter by reading joke books –
these are packed full of puns! Then use your new skills to
make up your own **hilarious** and pun-tastic jokes!

Gruesome GIANTS

If you've ever visited Giant Country, you'll already know that some of the beastliest characters ever are ... THE GIANTS. But you don't actually have to meet these beasts to know how mean they are. All you need to do is find out what they're called.

Bloodbottler

Bonecruncher

Childchewer

Fleshlumpeater

Now, look closer at these beastly names. (Use a magnifying glass if you like.) They are actually made up of two or more words stuck together!

For example:
CHILD + CHEWER = CHILDCHEWER.

The meanings of the words are combined too. (Gulp.) So if you see this particular giant . . . RUN. You don't want to be a giant's snack.

Gizzardgulper

Maidmasher

Manhugger

Meatdripper

Prepare for a once-in-a-lifetime opportunity to

NAME YOUR OWN GIANT.

Simply pick a word from the first list and
a word from the second list and glue them
together. If you're feeling really adventurous,
add brand new words to the lists and use
those instead to make giants that no one else
has ever thought of.

ADD ONE OF THESE

blood
bone
child
flesh
ghoul
gizzard
gore
man
meat
monster

+

TO ONE OF THESE

chomper
crusher
gulper
hugger
lumpeater
masher
smasher
splatter
squeezer
squisher

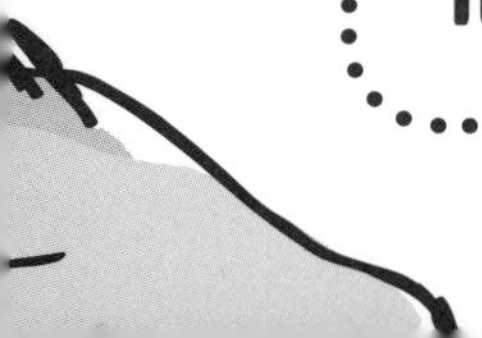

Giant WORDS

The word 'giant' is a **noun**. It means an imaginary* being that looks like a human, but is MUCH, MUCH BIGGER.

'Giants is all cannybully and murderful!
And they does gobble up human beans!'
— THE BFG

* Unless you've been to Giant Country, where they are obviously 100% real.

But the word 'giant' can also be an adjective, in which case it means **VERY, VERY BIG INDEED.**

Once again the giant peach was
sailing peacefully through the
mysterious moonlit sky.
— JAMES AND THE GIANT PEACH

54

Some words can be used as more than one word class (such as a noun, adjective, verb or adverb). If you ever want to find out what word class a word belongs to, simply look in a dictionary. You'll find the answer right next to every word.

GIANT *noun*
A giant is a huge humanlike creature found in traditional stories.

GIANT *adjective*
huge or enormous in size

Skrocks and SQUERKLES

Have you noticed how beastly beasts' names sound too? Some letters sound hard and scratchy, like the skr– at the beginning of skrock. But other letters are softer and bouncier like the bob– in bobolink. Which of these would you least like to bump into while travelling in a Great Glass Elevator?

'I tracked down **THE WHISTLE-PIG, THE BOBOLINK, THE SKROCK, THE POLLY-FROG, THE GIANT CURLICUE, THE STINGING SLUG AND THE VENOMOUS SQUERKLE** *who can spit poison right into your eye from fifty yards away.'*

— CHARLIE AND THE GREAT GLASS ELEVATOR

Skrock is the Swedish word for 'superstition'. Meanwhile, a curlicue is a decorative curl found in calligraphy. So if you ever want to invent an animal's name, remember that it's perfectly acceptable to look for inspiration ANYWHERE.

GRIMALKIN

CATTALOO

Both of these animals were found by Willy Wonka in his Great Glass Elevator. Can you guess whether they are real or make-believe . . . ?

Answers: They are both REAL. Grimalkin is an old-fashioned word for 'cat', while a cattaloo is a cross between a cow and a buffalo.

Are you bored of using the same old words? Then you need a mash-up! This is when chunks of existing words are mixed up to create brand-new ones!

Here's an easy one to start.

Switch **WHANGDOODLE** around to make . . . **DOODLEWANG!**

Now for something really clever!

Pick a real-life animal, like a **HIPPOPOTAMUS**.

Delve into the Greek myths to unearth a **GRIFFIN***.

Now stick them together! **HIPPOPOTAMUSGRIFFIN**.

Hmm. That's way too many letters. Let's lose a few!

HIPPO~~POTAMUSGR~~IFFIN

What's left? **HIPPOGRIFF!**

* A griffin is a mythical creature
with the head and wings of an eagle and the
body of a lion.

More mythical mash-ups!
CENTAUR – the upper body of a human and the lower body of a horse
HARPY – a mixture of a woman and a bird
MERMAID – a creature that is half-woman and half-fish

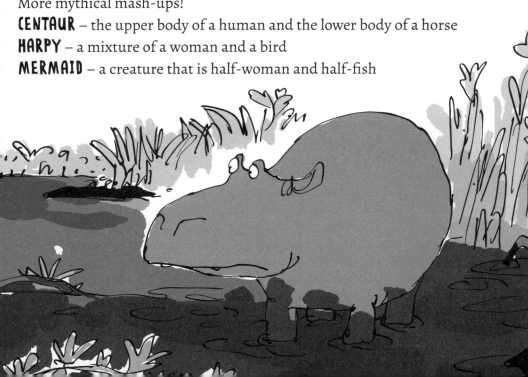

The BFG has discovered these extra-usual animals!
They've never been seen before! Or have they . . . ?

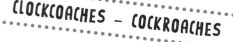

CROCKADOWNDILLIES – CROCODILES

HIPPODUMPLINGS – HIPPOPOTAMUSES

JIGGYRAFFES – GIRAFFES

NIGHTINGULLS – NIGHTINGALES

RHINOSTOSSTERISSES – RHINOCEROSES

What's your favourite animal? Is it a peacock or a platypus or a penguin or a pony? Pick one and then squiggle it and squish it until you've created a brand new name!

Phizz-whizzing fact

BFG is an **initialism**. This is an abbreviation made from the initial letters of other words, in this case, **Big Friendly Giant**. An initialism is different to an acronym, where the initial letters form a word, such as SCUBA (self-contained underwater breathing apparatus).

AND FINALLY...

Great whistling whangdoodles! You've reached the very last page of this **BEASTLY** – and also **BEWILDERING** – book. You've been on a zoological journey around the world of Roald Dahl and you've met many, many animals, both real and imaginary. What will you do now?!

DON'T PANIC. Roald Dahl didn't just write about animals. He wrote about all sorts of other things, too – such as **CHOCOLATE** and **CHIDDLERS** and **PEACHES** and **WITCHES**.

You can find all of these and **DILLIONS** more in the fantabulous Oxford *Roald Dahl Dictionary* . . .

. . . and of course in the phizz-whizzing poems and stories of ROALD DAHL.

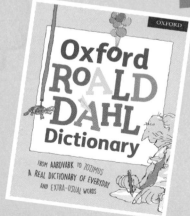